W9-ATS-759

TIGERS

Jean-Pierre Zwaenepoel

CHRONICLE BOOKS • SAN FRANCISCO

To my mother and the memory of my father and brother

Printed in Hong Kong.

Library of Congress Cataloging-in-Publication Data

Zwaenepoel, Jean-Pierre.

Tigers / Jean-Pierre Zwaenepoel ; introduction by Hashim Tyabji.

p. cm.

ISBN 0-8118-0136-5 (hc).—ISBN 0-8118-0143-8 (pb)

1. Tigers—India—Pictorial works. I. Title.

QL737.C23Z82 1992 91-44418

599.74′428—dc20 CIP

Book and cover design: Merrick Hamilton

Distributed in Canada by Raincoast Books,
112 East Third Avenue, Vancouver, B.C. V5T 1C8

10 9 8 7 6 5 4 3 2 1

Chronicle Books
275 Fifth Street
San Francisco, CA 94103

ACKNOWLEDGMENTS

I would like to thank H.S Pabla, R. Gopal and R.K. Singh, Field Directors of the Forest Department.

The generous help I received from three people was essential in producing this book: Hashim Tyabji, my 'jungle guru', who readily shared his knowledge and was also prepared to write the introduction; C. K. Murthy, who solved many problems; and not least E. A. Kuttappan, whose tireless and skillful tracking provided me with many opportunities to observe and photograph the tigers. I also benefited greatly from the efforts of Phul Singh, Sampath, Ramzan, Mantoo and Suklu.

I thank K. K. and Durgi Singh from the Bandhavgarh Jungle Camp for their hospitality. At this camp I was happy to share the campfire with Dushyant Singh, Dinesh Thapa, Avanti Mehta, Samantha Autie, Ted Kerasote, Thomas and Irmgard Wachtershauser and many guests during numerous discussions.

I am also grateful to John and Brenda Davies from Amersham (U. K.) and Patrick and Ria Hoet from Bruges (Belgium) for their support.

Finally, I hope this book may stress the necessity of finding a balance between the needs of man and of wild animals.

FOREWORD

Some years ago, while wandering through the forests of southern India, I happened to be staying with a forester who had been summoned to look into a reported case of a tiger cattle-lifting. As we bent to examine the slightly smudged imprints the tiger had left, my companion, a grizzled veteran with thirty years of service thickening his waist, shook his head ruefully: in all his years in the jungle he had never once seen a tiger in the wild. Plenty of signs, certainly, but nothing more. This is an extreme case that nevertheless serves to emphasize the elusiveness that lies at the very heart of the tiger's mystique. Sadly, a major cause of this elusiveness is a sheer lack of tigers. Over the past sixty years or so, the numbers have decreased to such an extent that the tiger has become less a reality than a legend.

Today, as we view the tiger barely managing to hold its own within its beleaguered redoubts, assailed from every direction by the pressures of human land hunger in all its manifestations, it is hard to imagine that the population of tigers was once so great that they were considered vermin to be exterminated at every opportunity. Tigers were never found in anywhere near the numbers that the bison reached on the plains of North America. Their pre-eminent position in the food chain as well as their forest habitat precluded that. Yet, in the minds of men, both animals were symbols *par excellence* of their respective habitats, and the reduction of their numbers to the present meager figures is a tragedy of comparable proportions. In the case of the tiger, the tragedy is compounded by the fact that this is no delicate creature confined to a narrow ecological ledge, susceptible to every minute shift in the environment, but a robust, adaptable beast requiring only adequate food, water, and cover to thrive in conditions that vary from semi-arid thorn forests to frigid Siberian evergreens.

Happily, it is still possible to go looking for tigers in the special reserves that have been set aside for them throughout the subcontinent over the past twenty years or so. For those who delight in the wilderness, there can be few more exciting or pleasurable ways of spending one's time than patiently stalking and following the most magnificent of cats in their jungle habitat.

It is essential, however, when setting off after a tiger, to equip oneself with a little humility. To be able to wander through tiger country must in itself be counted as a privilege; to catch even a fleeting glimpse of tiger must always be viewed as a bonus. Its preferred habitat is dense forest and lush grassland, a type of country that seriously inhibits visibility and into which the tiger, with its superb camouflage, melts with ease. No doubt there are many more man-sightings by tigers than vice-versa.

There are, however, some areas where tigers may be seen with greater ease and regularity than elsewhere. These are the remnants of the once-fabled forests of central India that have now been converted into national parks and sanctuaries. It was no accident that Kipling chose central India for the location of his *Jungle Book*. For this huge region, with its remote valleys and rugged hills forming a hard knot in the belly of India, has long been famous for the quantity and quality of its game. Even today, large tracts of this region retain a flavor of days past, when the jungle was dominant and human settlements hunkered down at the edge of the forest, their inhabitants wary of the depredations made upon crops and livestock and occasionally upon themselves by the creatures that dwelt in the wilderness hovering just beyond the firelight.

What makes these forests special for the tiger-tracker is not just that the forests abound in prey species, or that tiger populations reach optimum densities here, but rather that the forest is more open than in moister areas, the undergrowth not so dense, the grasses not quite so tall—all factors that greatly enhance "viewability." And it is not just the tiger that is more visible here but all the diverse fauna that constitute the pyramid, at the apex of which is the tiger. Nevertheless, patience, luck, and skill are prime requirements, and there are no guarantees. Indeed, a guaranteed tiger sighting would debase the very mystique that is such a large part of its attraction.

Of all the behavioral aspects of the tiger, its social life is perhaps the most fascinating. Often the question is asked whether an animal reputedly as solitary and reclusive as the tiger has much of a social life. The answer is that of course it must, if only to procreate! In fact, the tiger lives within a complex social system, interacting constantly, although not necessarily directly, with others of its kind. Its solitary habits, probably a response to a closed environment that favors the individual hunter over the pride, are not quite as deep-seated as previously thought. As the rapidly expanding tribe of tiger-watchers clocks in more hours of direct observation, new evidence of sustained association and social interaction has emerged.

Over the past few years, much has been learned about the tiger, and much yet remains to be learned. But, however much tiger lore and science we may compile, collate, and distill, the essence of the animal retains its fugitive quality, defying attempts to encapsulate it within the clumsy structure of words. The tiger elicits a deeply personal response from most people, touching some primal chord, for beyond the fact of its physical beauty, the tiger embodies all the majesty and mystery of the jungle.

Whether the various measures taken to arrest the tiger's decline will prove sufficient for the future, only time will tell. One thing is certain: if the tiger were ever to vanish, it would leave the forests bereft of color and drained of the vibrant energy, the magic sparkle that is the gift of the great predators.

Hashim Tyabji 1991

NOTE FROM THE AUTHOR

In the captions I have mentioned the names given by the *mahouts,* or elephant drivers, to those tigers we were able to observe for some length of time. It may sound odd or too familiar to name wild animals, but it served us a practical purpose, making identification easier. Perhaps it will also make their story more comprehensible.

Barka, which means "the big one," is the adult male. He took over the territory from a male who died of old age and porcupine quill infection in 1985. He probably fathered both of the litters I observed. On two occasions, I saw him seriously wounded. The second time he sustained a lame forepaw and started to depend on scavenging and stealing livestock for his survival. He was usually very tolerant toward the cubs, but would fight fiercely against intruders. On my last visit, he had become considerably weaker, and it is thought that he may not survive the monsoon, or that he will be pushed out of his territory by a younger male.

Sita, born in the monsoon of 1983, this cool-headed tigress took over her mother's territory. She mated with Barka in 1986. From her first litter, two cubs, Nar Bachcha (male) and Hardia (female), survived, and a third died. A new litter was born at the end of 1988. Again, three cubs were later seen, all of them male. One cub was later found dying of weakness; the other two, Dao and Balram, have started to lead independent lives. I saw Sita mating with Barka on my recent visit, in May 1991, and she may produce a new litter after the monsoon. However, there seems to be some intrusion on her territory by another female, Safeda.

Nar Bachcha, which means "the male cub," was born out of Sita's first litter. On my first visit, January to May 1988, I witnessed his gradual separation from his mother. Later, he was occasionally seen in an adjacent territory. There is a chance he might become the next ruler of Barka's territory, in which case he should be given a new name, appropriate for his new dignity.

Hardia, named so after the area where she has settled, is the sister of Nar Bachcha. She has always been shy and furtive. After she left her mother's territory during the monsoon of 1988, she disappeared until earlier this year when she was seen and photographed with three small cubs.

Dao, a male cub from Sita's second litter, was born at the end of 1988. He got his name, which means "older brother," because he appeared to dominate his brother, Balram. Another male cub from the same litter was found abandoned, and he later died from weakness. Dao was still frequenting his mother's territory in May 1991. One morning he even chased Sita from a sambar kill. He is mostly on his own now, though he has been seen being friendly with Balram.

(Above) Half-submerged in a jungle stream, Barka cools off after a territorial dispute with another male.

Balram is more playful and extroverted than Dao, always responding first to his mother's calls or seeking her attention. Bold though he is, he seems less aware of danger than Dao. He would sometimes follow or playfully stalk an elephant, making a game of trying to catch its twitching tail. Like Dao, he was still using Sita's beat in May 1991.

Safeda is an elderly female who started to show up in parts of Sita's home range. Her origin is not known, but she may have been ousted from an adjacent area. At first it was thought that she would push Sita out, as she was the larger and more muscular of the two. She actually has the appearance of a male. The presence of Dao, Balram, and Safeda seemed to put Sita under much stress when she was in heat prior to mating with Barka in May 1991.

For a short time, I could also follow a tigress with two cubs, a male and female, in Kanha National Park. A year later, I heard that the tigress had died, and that the cubs later had died, probably from starvation. Some of their pictures appear in these pages.

INTRODUCTION

A man cub is a man's cub, and he must learn all the laws of the jungle.
—Baloo the bear in *The Jungle Book,* by Rudyard Kipling

Of all India's mysteries, it was the idea that somewhere, far away from the crowded, bustling cities, an elusive tiger still lurked in patches of untamed wilderness that lured me back after my first short visit in the Spring of 1987. Back home in Belgium, books had taught me that, naturally cautious and evasive, tigers like to spend most of the day concealed in thick forests or slumbering in tall grasslands. So when I returned to India in the winter of the same year, hoping to catch a glimpse of this almost mystical predator and not exactly sure where to go, I knew I had not committed myself to an easy challenge. Yet, it only took one encounter with a tiger in the wild to turn my initial interest into obsession. My plan to continue my travels along the Silk Road and to Europe with the Transsiberian Express were easily abandoned. Soon I was to find myself in the Indian jungle whenever I could afford, each time making the most of the six months my visa allowed me to stay.

It was in a remote national park, hidden from people's attention among the rugged Vindhya hills in central India, that I would have the opportunity to fulfill my dream of following a few tigers for a length of time. Bandhavgarh, a flat-topped hill that lends its name to the area, dominates the dramatic scenery. Like a tiger, it emanates legendary strength. For many centuries, people found a safe, natural fort here. Once a center of human activity, Bandhavgarh served as the capital of the ancestors of the present maharaja of Rewa until 1617. Later, the fortress grew increasingly deserted. Nature took over and sloth bear, leopard, and tiger made their home in the temples and numerous dug-out caves that littered the steep slopes. Later, this jungle became a *shikar* or hunting reserve for the royal family and its guests. In 1968, the game reserve was handed over to the state of Madhya Pradesh to be turned into a national park. Though in itself only 168 square miles (437 sq. km), Bandhavgarh National Park is well connected to other tracts of contiguous wilderness.

(Left) Unconcerned, a little green bee-eater is on the lookout for winged insects.

In and outside the park, stretches of tall, straight sal trees dominate on dry land. These stately trees are seldom leafless and usually lack dense undergrowth, hence they give off the feeling of an open, cool woodland. Bamboo jungle prevails amid boulders and rocky outcrops of soft sandstone on the many hillocks. On the upper slopes, sal and bamboo give way to mixed forest. This type of woodland becomes dry and bare during the hot season (May/June), forcing animals to descend in search of water and pasture.

Interspersed in the valleys are grassy meadows. Some of these clearings used to be small villages with cultivated fields. Since the area was established as a national park, a few remaining hamlets have been relocated after delicate negotiations. Today, these open meadows are the stages on which the natural confrontation between deer, antelope, and carnivores unfolds.

For tracking and following tigers in swampy grasslands or through dense jungle scrub on a hilly terrain, no vehicle could be more effective than a trained elephant. Tigers and elephants will usually avoid each other's company, but have now come to tolerate one another. Some cats are tracked by the *mahouts* since cubhood and have ceased to run away and have begun to ignore these giant backpackers. When discovered, tigers have, step by step, allowed me, on elephantback, to get an intimate view of their mysterious practices. Yet, to see one is never a sure bet. Patience and good luck are essential. When they are tolerant, we can sometimes watch them for hours on end. At other times we might not see the tips of their tails, even after several days of meticulous tracking, as though they had vanished altogether. Only a jigsaw puzzle of pugmarks on the ground from their nocturnal wanderings or a sudden outburst of distant alarmcalls will give us a clue as to their whereabouts.

The area the *mahouts* search as a daily routine is tailor made for a tigress raising her cubs. On my first visit in the winter of 1987-88, I observed the gradual separation of a family. Initially, Sita's two nearly full-grown cubs, Nar Bachcha and Hardia, still joined their mother on her foraging outings as apprentice hunters. Born during the monsoon of 1983, Sita grew to become the matriarch, claiming rights to this prime tiger country, abundant with prey, cover, and water, from her mother.

(Right) Kuttapan rides his tusker, Gautham, through tall grasses in their daily search for tigers.

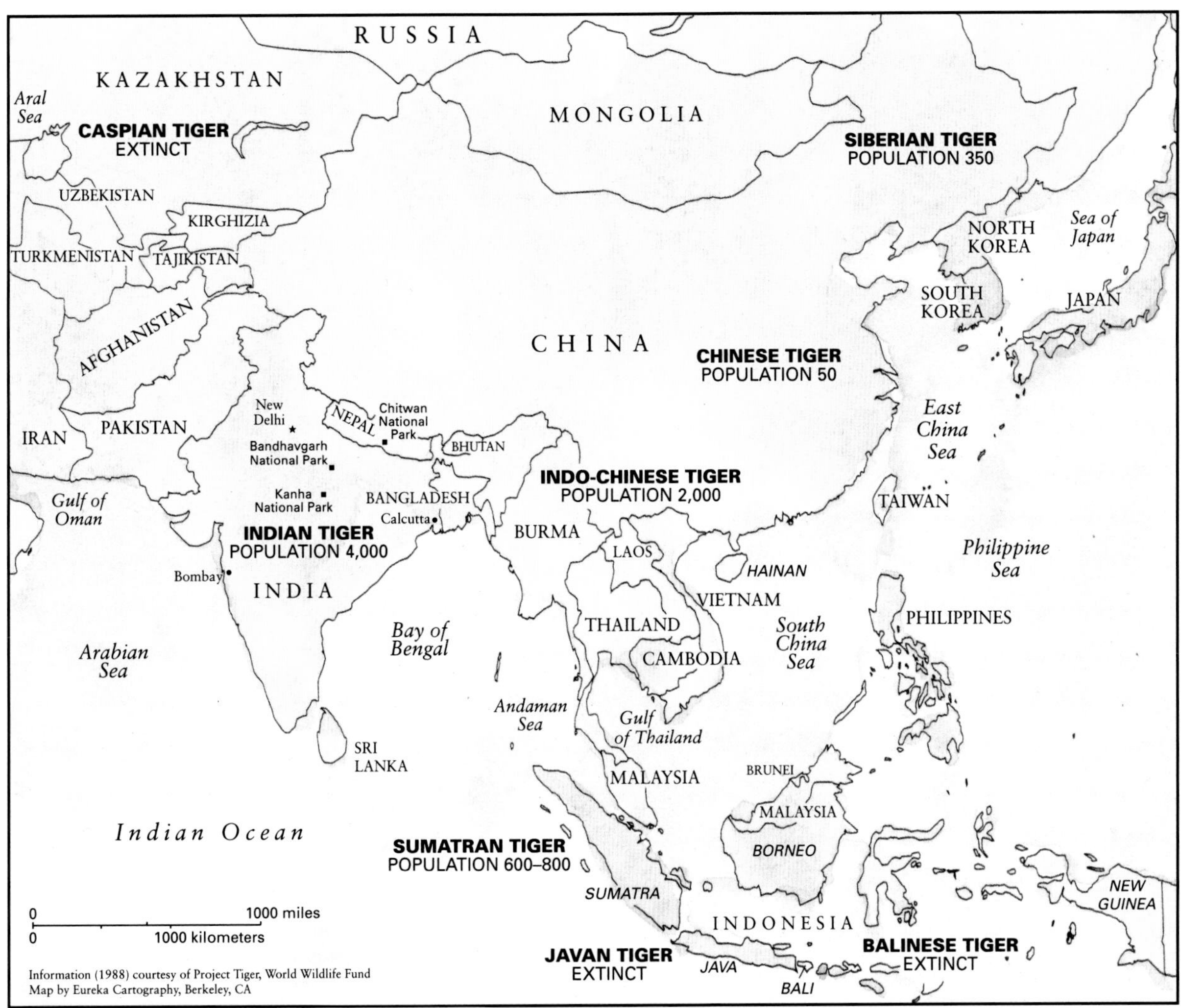

(Above) Long ago, the tiger was distributed across much of Asia. Dispersing from the north by the late Pleistocene period, the tiger evolved into eight subspecies. By the turn of the century it was thought that some 40,000 Indian tigers lived in the jungle. Today, the Balinese, Caspian, and Javan tiger are extinct. The Chinese tiger is struggling to make it into the next century with the help of a captive breeding program. Except for maybe the Siberian tiger, the remaining subspecies all range in densely populated countries, where one can easily forecast a rapid depletion of available forest resources. Because of this sharp increase in human pressure on the environment and over-hunting, India, Nepal, and the World Wildlife Fund launched "Project Tiger" in 1972, which endeavored to protect wild habitats throughout the Indian subcontinent. The tiger populations in these national parks are slowly rebounding, and a host of other animals, like the Asian elephant and the Indian rhino, have also profited from the tiger's endangered status.

(Above) Barka and Sita about to mate, as seen from elephantback. In tall grasslands and thick forests in hilly terrain, tiger tracking and, when lucky, watching is most effective from a trained elephant.

(Above) Bathing in golden light, mahouts *(elephant drivers) steer their elephants through tall grasslands. Examining tiger imprints, interpreting alarm calls and nervous game, and watching the commotion of scavengers, these trackers rely on intuition and sheer luck to bring them face to face with "Shere Khan," Kipling's name for the tiger.*

(Right) Hardia looks bored and drowsy in the absence of her mother. Her brother passes time between his mother's visits by working his oversized paws with his rough tongue. Small cubs are taught to stay put when their mother is out on a hunt. Initially, they will remain close to each other for comfort.

Throughout this territory, the family has a range of favorite vantage points where they liked to laze in the daytime. But even while resting, Sita and her cubs constantly swiveled their ears one at a time, like the eyes of a chameleon, to scan the jungle for signs of a possible meal: the sound of rustling leaves revealing a herd of *chital*, or spotted deer, shuffling under a fruit-laden tree; the bellowing of the solitary, elk-like sambar that remained well hidden in deep cover; the noisy grunts of a sounder of rooting wild boar. Once, when the sun had just set, a group of tourists watched the tiger clan work as a team to kill a large sambar doe.

As the days passed, however, tension slowly developed between the mother and her cubs. The first signs of irritation surfaced as quarrels over food. A 600-pound sambar stag now lasted only two days between the three tigers.

Communal hunting and food sharing seems to be less effective for a stalking predator that relies on cover than for "runners," predators developed and built to run, who chase their prey in packs, like wild dogs. One evening we watched Sita threaten and aggressively charge her own offspring, approaching the confused cubs in the same way she would prey. We deduced that she was making it clear to them that the time had come for the cubs to disperse and explore new hunting grounds. Or perhaps she was teaching her young a lesson in aggressive behavior, a vital part of their education in surviving the hardships of life in the jungle.

Not a week later, we followed Sita along a trail. She appeared to be restless and preoccupied. Long-ranging, plaintive roars alerted the jungle to her presence. We watched her spray low bushes and prominent tree trunks four different times: She obviously wanted male company. Distressed and

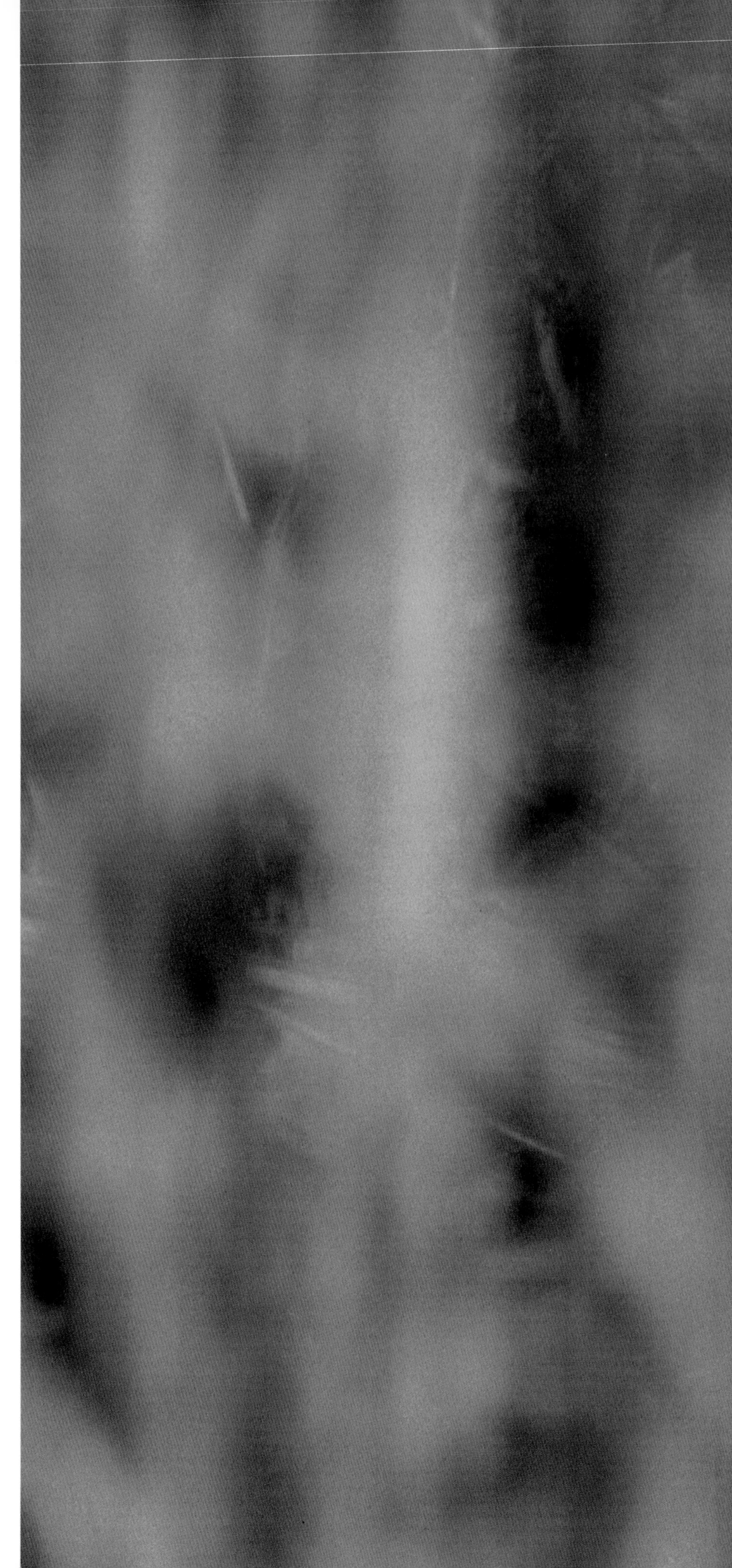

(Right) A portrait of Sita reflects her assertive personality. Said to be born during the monsoon of 1983, Sita later claimed her own mother's territory. From Sita's first litter, only two—Nar Bachcha (male) and Hardia (female)—survived, and a third died. A new litter of three cubs was born at the end of 1988, all of them male. One cub later died, apparently of weakness. The other two, Dao and Balram, had left their mother by the summer of 1991.

left to fend for themselves, the newly independent young adults fell on hard times. Careless while stalking and inexperienced in killing techniques, their attempts to hunt down large prey invariably failed. They relied heavily on scavenging and killing small game to survive this critical stage in their lives. Once, we met the timid female, Hardia, with a few porcupine quills embedded in her neck and mouth. These spear-like spines can disable a tiger, sometimes with fatal results.

In November 1988, I again accompanied Kuttappan, a *mahout* with whom I share a passion for the big cats. Each year, the park closes during and after the monsoon as forest roads become impassable. I was anxious to catch up on the events in Sita's family. Quite pleased with my first series of slides, I had decided to take a prolonged leave from my job as a land-surveyor and armed myself with wider and longer lenses. Nar Bachcha's distinctive imprints were now plotted over a large tract, suggesting he was traveling more widely. He had become a proficient hunter, quite capable of tackling large and potentially dangerous prey, like a large sambar stag or wild boar with razor-sharp tusks. Although fully grown in size now, it would still take him another two and a half years to acquire the determined look of a mature male. Hardia, too, had drifted away south of her natal area. She was seen again in the spring of 1991 by Hashim Tyabji, a friend and naturalist who studies these tigers. Proudly emerging from the tall grasses, she had three youngsters trotting around her.

Around Christmas 1988, Sita's daily routine of retreating among the many rocky crevices and caves, as well as the sight of her swollen nipples, revealed that she had delivered her second litter. Like all mothers with newly born young, she acted extremely cautious and nervous. She carefully moved the den every so often to avoid detection from other predators and to rid themselves of parasites and insects. Born and raised in this territory, Sita had each animal trail, well-located look-out, permanent water hole, and safe hideaway mapped out in her mind—a valuable asset when rearing vulnerable cubs.

Only occasionally would she allow us a brief glimpse of her new offspring. I could hardly contain my excitement when I spotted the three cute kittens, no bigger than domestic cats, waddling around on floppy paws. Only the faint rustle of leaves betrayed their presence. Other times, we heard only their high-pitched, fragile voices. Scattered and seemingly lost in dense and tall grassland, they meowed desperately for their mother's security. We later determined that Sita had produced an all-male litter.

We assumed the resident male, who we nicknamed Barka, or "the big one," may have fathered Sita's two litters. He was a good-sized adult in his prime. Barka proved to be a remarkable tiger. In 1985, he appropriated the vacant territory of another male who had died from the uncomfortable combination of old age and imbedded porcupine quills. Based on years of critical examinations of pugmarks, Hashim Tyabji had managed to map Barka's extensive territory. It overlapped the established territories of three females he knew of, including Sita.

Field studies of tigers' social systems in Royal Chitwan National Park, Nepal, and Kanha National Park, India, suggest that tigers space themselves so that breeding individuals have exclusive access to areas with high prey densities. In these core areas, mothering females tend to outnumber adult males by about three to one. This spacing pattern allows more tigresses to raise their young under optimal conditions, while also restricting the number of tigers hunting in that area. Competition forces non-breeding males and females to disperse into adjacent forests holding less game, which are often forests along the periphery of the tiger reserves. There, some tigers wait for a vacancy, sharing the land with peasants, tribal communities, and their livestock. Others move on, migrating like nomadic wanderers. Although a tigress that prowls in peripheral areas may also become pregnant, her chances of raising cubs to adulthood could be slim due to insufficient natural prey and shelter or competition with man.

To maintain their territorial rights, resident tigers have to regularly patrol and stake out their territory. Between females, territorial behavior seems to be based on competition for food and a safe place to raise cubs.

It is important to add here that one cannot always speculate that tigers are spaced out accordingly, as their behavior can differ markedly depending on their circumstances. I observed that tigers are highly individual, quite often unpredictable animals, each blessed with personal traits. It should be no surprise then that variations to this social system, like pride behavior, may emerge from different studies and evolve as future generations of tigers adapt to a changing habitat.

One dramatic day in April of 1989 we came across Barka, his eyes were glazed and his face was drenched in blood. He sat partly submerged in the Charanganga, a perennial stream in the heart of Sita's home range and a cool resting spot on hot and oppressive days. Less than thirty yards away and partly covered by a bamboo clump, we spied another huge male, much heavier in the neck and shoulders. Not moving an inch or even twisting an ear, both warriors stared fiercely at each other for nearly ten minutes. Occasionally Barka would lick his face with a painful grimace.

Since no gathering of jungle crows or a spiral cloud of soaring vultures heralded a kill, we could only guess they were engaged in a territorial dispute. We watched breathlessly to see what would happen. Surprisingly, as he *appeared* less wounded than Barka, the intruder retreated from the area submissively—moments later he had vanished.

The next morning we tracked Barka again, who was still in a daze. His left cheek had been ripped open in combat, exposing pink flesh and jaw bones. Though tigers have a well-developed system of communication, (like territorial marking) to avoid such antagonistic confrontations, fatal clashes between tigers of the same sex have been recorded. Unable to keep the gaping wound clean with his long tongue, Barka wouldn't have survived for long if nature had been left to take its course. One can argue that human beings should not interfere in such a case, but officials of the Forest Department considered the potential danger of having a severely wounded tiger lingering close to areas of human habitation too high. In 1981 a male tiger, maddened by a wound to his head, had claimed several lives in a nearby village before he could be destroyed.

The officials decided to tranquilize Barka and to monitor him closely afterwards. Once he was darted and drugged, the festering injury was cleaned and stitched. Luckily, his impressive set of canines and carnassials was intact, and later Barka fully recovered. His survival may well have saved Sita's cubs too. A newly established male is likely to try to kill small cubs and oust larger ones within the territory he overtakes so he can speed up the tigress' readiness to mate and spread his own genes, rather than investing time and energy in defending unrelated cubs. Similar behavior has been documented in lions and primates.

While Barka was recovering, Sita hunted with great efficiency to satisfy

(Right) Barka bares his magnificent set of canines while yawning.

(Above) Balram rests on a rock.

her ever-demanding cubs. When a kill was too far away or too heavy to drag to the safety of the lair, she simply journeyed with the now-mobile cubs to a secluded hideaway near the feeding site. Cautiously guarded by their mother, the cubs were allowed to gorge themselves in quick turns, in case another hungry predator was drawn to the appetizing spot.

On a hot premonsoon afternoon, as he later told me, Kuttappan watched the family relaxing near a puddle. When they left at dusk, the smallest of the three cubs remained seemingly fast asleep near the waterline. As it did not respond to its mother's nudging and low moaning, Sita had no choice but to abandon her cub. Realizing something was amiss and worried that the cub may drown if left there, Kuttappan got down from his elephant, Gautham, and took the unconscious cub to camp for treatment. It died a few days later. Too weak, the baby tiger could not compete with his energetic, better-developed litter-mates. Natural selection ensures that only the fittest survive. It is estimated that, in the wild, less than half of the tiger cubs reach adulthood.

Sita did not mourn for long, for the other cubs needed every ounce of her maternal care. Although virtually weaned by now, they would still occasionally nestle her belly and try to suckle when they were hungry.

All young cats are fond of games, and these tiger cubs were no different. When they were about seven months old, the two brothers had begun to

investigate their home habitat with great enthusiasm. Both siblings were particularly fascinated by moving objects. A branch that swayed in a breeze was caught and chewed; lizards were chased in hot pursuit over sandstone boulders; and bright butterflies were vainly pawed at until they finally gave up.

The boys had also learned to interpret the sounds of the jungle. They became visibly alerted and excited when distant alarm calls suggested that their mother might be on the prowl. Upon her arrival, Sita was invariably greeted and nuzzled with great excitement, especially when the cubs smelled fresh meat. Gentle grooming and frolicking sealed their obvious affection. Reassured to have their mother home, the cubs would chase and tease each other with heightened intensity. Encouraging their boisterous games, Sita often lashed out her tail like a striking cobra. Both cubs would respond instantly to her invitation with a sudden rush, grabbing the curling tail between their oversized paws. Once all excess energy had been burned up, the young cats would settle closely to their mother and curl up for a peaceful nap. It was while watching the games and pranks of these two cubs that I wondered what a handicap it must be for a single cub to grow up alone. All that tugging and squabbling with one another serves to polish a tiger's natural predatorial skills—a sizable advantage in the competitive world of the forest.

After observing these cubs for a period of time, we started to recognize some distinguishing features. The *mahouts* christened the extrovert cub Balram, which refers to Lord Krishna's brother. Balram was close to his mother and usually the first to greet her. Bold and curious, he often returned our attention by displaying his intense interest in the elephant's ever-twitching tail and flapping ears. Surely he did not think Gautham was inviting him for a game of tail catching? Yet it was the other cub, marked by his furtive and suspicious behavior, that seemed to be dominant. We named him Dao or "older brother." He was the first to venture out on his own for short exploring journeys.

The two young cubs were a joy to watch. Their ever-changing facial expressions were most captivating. One could see their mood swing from playful to bored, from gregarious to threatening, or from sleepy to fully alert. I found their rich repertoire of body postures and subtle language of facial expressions amazing for an animal labeled a nocturnal loner.

(Left) Tormented by pestering flies, Balram shakes his head.

A year after the all-out fight I witnessed, Barka was again in trouble. This time a patch of flesh had been bitten from his foreleg. Only constant licking prevented the injury from becoming infected.

Not a month later, we spotted Barka and Sita together. At first we thought this was just another fleeting visit, but then we saw Sita slowly rise and stretch her lean, lithe body. Emitting a friendly puffing sound and

(Above) Cold winter mist enshrouds the forest that Rudyard Kipling chose as the setting for his fantasy stories in The Jungle Book.

sliding her tail sensually alongside his flanks, she circled around Barka invitingly. They rubbed heads and shoulders to confirm their bond. Visibly hampered by his severe limp, Barka grabbed Sita with a gentle nape bite and straddled her. He maintained his loose grip on Sita's neck fur while they mated briefly. The jungle reverberated when they released each other in an explosion of snarls and growls. We were both amazed and puzzled: it is considered most unusual for a tigress to mate while she is still caring for a largely dependent litter, especially since there had been no territorial takeover by a male. For five days the couple stayed together, entwined in intimacy. Sita was frequently the aggressor initiating the mating ritual, which occurred as often as every ten to thirty minutes.

One night I could hear the couple's noisy love games from my room. Early next morning, no more than 500 yards away, we found Barka near the remains of a cow that had strayed into the park. Although Sita stayed by the kill for a while, she was not allowed to share in it.

Because Barka's paw never properly healed he was handicapped and forced to rob other carnivores of their quarry or to take cattle grazing along the fringes of the forest to survive. Increased confrontations over food put Barka's life in danger; and although the government now pays farmers for livestock killed by predators outside the park boundary, leopards and tigers are still deliberately poisoned by pesticides.

One year later I was back in the forest. It was the summer of 1991 and the air was uncomfortably warm and heavy. Bamboo had shed their leaves in the dry heat, but despite better visibility, we still had to struggle to keep up with Dao. Striding purposefully, only pausing now and then to catch some scent or to locate a sound we could not hear, Dao drew us deeper and deeper into the ravine where we had watched Sita near a half-eaten sambar doe the day before.

We stopped short at the sudden thunderous sound of coughing roars. Beyond our view, two tigers clashed over the kill behind a jumble of rocks. Once silence was restored, Sita emerged, deprived of her quarry. Taking no risks, and already well-fed, she had given in. Dao, the pirate, had confirmed his dominance. My own observations suggest that it is not uncommon for these tigers to gather near a large kill. Barka, an accomplished opportunist, seems to be especially skilled at detecting putrefying carcasses.

I first caught sight of the elderly tigress called Safeda through my binoculars. Muscular and almost the size of a male, she had repeatedly been seen in parts of Sita's well-defined territory over the last few months. Evasive or aggressive on former encounters, she was resting after cooling off in a muddy pool. We waited patiently to win her confidence. Once she realized that we posed no threat, I was happy to take her first identifying pictures. Through my telelens I could see that swarming flies were clus-

(Right) After cleaning himself meticulously, Balram peers around for prey, sniffing the late afternoon air.

tered on her scarred nose. The yellowish-brown color of her worn teeth and a broken canine confirmed Hashim's suspicion that she was possibly past breeding age and had been ousted from her own territory. Or was she encroaching on Sita's home?

Only three days later, we tracked Safeda again in tall grass. This time, Sita was nearby. Tense with her ears pricked, Sita monitored Safeda's position and every move she made. When they inevitably came face to face, Sita quickly lowered herself and snarled, baring her teeth and flattening her ears. Ultimately Sita withdrew, avoiding a direct physical confrontation.

A few days before the first tropical storms brought relief to the sun-baked land, we encountered Sita in a meadow. A patch of skin had been torn from her back. Had she met Safeda again? Sita later slipped quietly into a cool cave, carved out on the slopes of the fort. According to some Sanskrit inscriptions, it may have sheltered humans since A. D. 300. Was she already checking for a safe place to give birth, or was she just seeking relief from the searing heat?

Dao and Balram, now two and a half years old, had gone their separate ways months earlier. Both were still frequenting Sita's home range, but each was greeted with a stern glance and much hissing and spitting by its mother. The days when Sita would cuddle and groom her cubs were long gone. Although neither male was an accomplished hunter yet, Dao and Balram appeared fit and well, set to become powerful adults.

It was obvious that it caused Sita much stress to cohabit with Safeda, Dao, and Balram. As an old old Chinese proverb says: "One hill cannot hold two tigers." They were all competing for food now, and soon she might start regularly losing kills to any of them—not a calming prospect if she had to raise a new litter in the near future.

Again, it was Sita's restless behavior and repeated territorial marking that indicated she was in heat. Ten days later Barka caught her signal and appeared. But somehow it was sad to watch this jungle veteran with his faded coat. His handicap had worn him out, and we doubted whether he would survive the approaching monsoon.

In 1972 India, Nepal, and the World Wildlife Fund launched "Project Tiger." For reasons largely related to a sharp increase in human pressure on the environment (and overhunting), the number of tigers in the wild had fallen dramatically. Based on an ecosystem approach, a variety of wild habitats throughout the Indian subcontinent were turned into protected areas. The tiger population rebounded well and a decade later its numbers appeared to be stable. As a bonus, samples of pristine forest were preserved and a host of other animals profited from the tiger's endangered status. Traveling the undulating plains in a packed train, I wondered how a country that contained a human population of nearly 900 million and an enormous number of livestock still manages to set aside enough wilderness for an animal like the tiger that needs plenty of space. It remains to be seen, despite the striking success of Project Tiger, whether the tiger has been guaranteed a place to roam free for generations to come.

In bygone days, the tiger was distributed across much of Asia. Today, except for the Siberian tiger, the remaining subspecies all live in densely populated countries, where one can easily predict the ever-increasing exploitation of the available forest resources. This can only lead to one thing: a growing conflict between commercial logging, conservation, and human interests.

Analysis of census figures reveals that as many as two-thirds of the pos-

(Right) On top of a hillock and well hidden from airborne scavengers, Barka is finishing off a sambar doe which has kept him occupied here for the last few days. He took over this hilly territory from a male who died of old age and porcupine quills in 1985.

(Right) Bold and curious, Balram usually gives the impression of being carefree and unaware of danger. He was the extrovert cub from Sita's second litter, born at the end of 1988. He left his mother by May 1991, but was still seen frequenting her territory months later.

(Above) Born and brought up in this prime tiger land, Sita had gradually become accustomed to the elephants. Their occasional presence did not seem to disturb her or to affect her behavior as a wild ranging animal, as she was mainly active at night. Sometimes while tending her cubs, she would suddenly walk off, leaving her offspring in our company as a proof of her trust. Animal psychologists think that the tiger sees the human on elephantback as an additional, albeit probably strange, limb.

sibly overestimated 4,000 wild tigers in India may live outside the protection of a national park. These tigers live in constant danger in a habitat subject to human overexploitation.

The lack of soil conservation, combined with overgrazing, uncontrolled forest fires, and an ever-growing demand for timber, has already turned (or are in the process of turning) large tracts of unprotected forests into disturbed scrub. Unlike leopards, tigers cannot adapt to such a depleted habitat. Once degraded forests lose the ability to sustain a healthy deer population (or other wildlife), tigers are likely to come into direct conflict with man and his domestic stock.

In April 1989 I had the chance to experience firsthand the effects of forcing tigers and humans into such close proximity. I was staying with friends overnight in an idyllic spot called Parsuli on our way to a remote farm. Before sunset, we went out for a stroll in the nearby forest. Walking through a *nallah,* or dry stream bed, we noticed the distant smell of putrefying meat. We then detected the pugmarks of a tigress. They looked small and fresh. We cautiously proceeded, when only 200 yards farther, we froze. Tiger! Hardly a short stone's throw away, yet almost invisible in the faint light of dusk, we saw the back of the tigress; she was lapping up water between bouts of feeding on her kill. It is rare to come upon a tiger when it is unaware of being watched by man. Still, it did not take us long to decide it was safer to climb our way out of the *nallah.* Our escape was betrayed when dry leaf litter crunched under our nervous feet. As surprised as we were, the tigress snarled viciously, leapt to the other side of the *nallah* and returned to her quarry. We hurried back on shaking legs for our own dinner.

Even under the best circumstances, coexistence between man and large predators is always critical. Once too much pressure is exerted on the habitat on which both depend, it becomes inevitable that one of the parties has got to go. Usually, it is the big cat that is the loser. To safeguard a viable tiger population and to minimize conflicts with man, conservationists therefore stress the need to maintain, or to restore, a buffer of secondary forests around tiger sanctuaries to ensure its survival.

It is thought that most tiger havens have become too small and too isolated, like islands in a sea of human activity. Trapped in such small pockets for their long-term survival, young dispersing tigers are increasingly prevented from pairing up with distant, unrelated cats. Wildlife biologists fear that, as a result, continued inbreeding may erode their genetic diversity with catastrophic consequences in the future.

On the other hand, peasants and tribal communities living near tiger reserves will argue that they have hardly benefitted from conservation efforts. They wonder why wild animals they consider harmful or dangerous should be given legal protection, while at night they have to guard their precious crops and livestock against raiders from the jungle.

Destruction of habitats takes its toll in other ways as well. While walking on land adjoining the park, I once came upon a group of people camping under a mohwa tree. They were Bansore people, a subcaste also known as "bamboo weavers." These tribals lead a semi-nomadic life, harvesting bamboo in a forest from which they make baskets or other house hold items. After selling these handiworks in villages and markets, they move on to another forest. These days, however, they are being forced to walk ever farther to collect bamboo.

India has a treasure of such tribes, whose traditional and often unique lifestyles are deeply rooted in the jungle. To lose them would be a cultural disaster. So eventually, both man and beast suffer from environmental degradation.

In developing countries, the greatest challenge in saving wildlife may well be to understand and improve the living conditions of the rural communities along the edges of the wilderness areas. Without their active participation, all management schemes are bound to fail.

Nature is plentiful with symbiotic relationships. In the Indian jungle, langur monkeys and spotted deer complement each others' defense systems against the big predators. Will we be able to strike a mutually beneficial balance between human and wildlife conservation interests? Solving this question may determine whether future generations will be fortunate enough to marvel at the sight or sound of a wild tiger.

(Right) Perched high up on the slopes of Bandhavgarh fort, reminding one of an eagle in its nest, Sita surveys the surrounding jungle for the movement of game. Three young cubs, around three months old, look bewildered by the size of the elephant intruding on their private world near the den. For weeks, her tracks led us to a maze of rocky crevices and caves littering the hill-side, which indicated that she had recently given birth to a new litter. Our suspicions were confirmed later when we saw her swollen nipples as she fed on a kill.

(Above) Balram has climbed his way into a tree and peers through a screen of foliage. A fully grown tiger is too heavy to feel comfortable in a tree, but occasionally, small cubs have been seen to climb up one when startled, or when they want to explore.

(Right) Having almost no natural enemies, the tiger stands at the apex of the food chain in the Indian jungle. When this habitat declines, the big cat may well disappear long before other species are affected. These young cats, however, are unaffected by this problem. They are absorbed with investigating their environment, and to them, the elephants are a most intriguing element of it. Nar Bachcha and Balram are often mesmerized by the elephant's swaying trunk constantly reaching for tender bamboo, its flapping ears, and ever-flagging tail. Here, Nar Bachcha may want to provoke the elephant in a game of 'king of the castle', or may merely be curious about the strange creatures atop its back.

(Above) Sita emerges from a jumble of rocks, setting out to prowl throughout the night. Born and brought up in this wild country, she knows of a range of impenetrable fortresses that make ideal dens to hide vulnerable cubs. A tigress may stay with her newborn kittens for the first few days but must then leave to find food. Only later, when they can be of any help, will a tigress encourage her cubs to join in on her foraging trips.

(Above) A tigress enjoys a short catnap. Knowing her cubs are safely cocooned in a burrow, she can relax.

(Above) In 1988, I observed this male and female cub in Kanha National Park, a vast and famous tiger reserve in Central India. They were about six to seven months old. The male cub had very unusual markings on his forepaws. When I returned a year later, I was told that their mother had died of unknown causes. Unable to hunt for themselves yet, both cubs had presumably met the same fate.

(Above) As day dawns, Sita crosses a meadow on her way back to the slopes of Bandhavgarh fort to tend her cubs. Some of these clearings were once villages with cultivated fields in a bygone past.

(Left) Reunited, Sita, Dao, and Balram reveled in their ritual of nuzzling, rubbing heads and bodies, and social grooming. Here, Sita licks Dao's ear. This mutual cleaning generally suggests a relaxed mood and helps to tighten the bond between a mother and her cubs.

(Above) A tigress and her young male cub lie digesting, heads together in affection, on a comfortable mattress of grass. Meanwhile, the female cub, well hidden, has her bout of feeding on a chital stag.

(Above) Their woolly coat and long tail wet by a sudden downpour, common langur huddle together for shelter. An infant remains barely visible. It has been observed among common langur that, shortly after birth, mothers pass their newborn infants to other members as an introduction to the troop.

(Above) As the light of another steamy hot summer day in Kanha National Park fades away, a tigress takes her offspring for a refreshing dip and drink in a shallow jungle pool. Their confidence boosted by having their mother so close, the cubs quickly break into a boisterous game of mudwrestling, which tests their strength. In a few weeks, with the onset of the monsoon, this place will be flooded once again.

(Left) As part of his learning process, Balram practices his biting skills by chewing and nibbling a twig.

(Right) A gaur bull lifts its massive head to allow an agile black drongo to pick insects from its humid nostrils. In the dry season, the shy gaur come down from the seclusion of the wooded hills in search of water and pasture. Although an unprotected gaur calf may be attacked, a bull like this, weighing as much as 1,600 pounds, has little to fear from tiger predation.

(Above) Ears cocked, Dao and Balram have picked up Sita's low contact call on her return.

(Above and right) Daring Balram playfully stalks Barka, who rests near the chital carcass he robbed from Sita. Balram may be intending to retrieve his mother's kill, or simply playing with his father's tail. It does not matter to Barka. Upset by this intrusion, he erupts, teeth bared to reprimand the cub. Suddenly scared, Balram quickly bows in respect, rolling over on his back to show his submission, and the skirmish is settled.

(Right) After preening and shaking off loose, snow-like feathers, an egret returns to its roosting tree on clean wings.

(Above) Her long, sensory whiskers bristling, Sita stretches her slender body as she sets off to hunt under cover of the night.

(Above) The sun steadily disappears in the fork of a bare mohwa tree.

(Above) As the summer sun drops behind a hillock, Balram, on his own now, tosses his head to test a warm, sudden breeze.

(Above) Barka, in his prime, jumps across a brooklet with feline grace; his round stomach and scars are reminders of a fight he had with Nar Bachcha over a kill.

(Right) A wide, fierce-looking yawn exposes Dao's prime, dagger-like canines. Combined with his rectable claws, they help him to get a quick and lethal grip on his prey. Set at the back of the jawbones is another pair of strong sharp teeth called the carnassials. These serve to cut meat and crush bones. The condition and color of a tiger's teeth give a good idea of its age.

(Above) A leopard bounds forward, exploding like a released spring. Basically, tigers and leopards use the same hunting techniques: a surprise attack is their key to success. Once potential prey is spotted, both predators still must stalk to within a short distance to strike. Although each is superbly adapted for such strenuous attacks, most trials end in failure.

(Above) Nar Bachcha meanders through a maze of dead bamboo. Tigers usually walk in dense forests where game is often scattered, and a lonely stalker must actively move about to detect a possible meal. Although it can grow to be the size of a tree, bamboo belongs in fact to the grass family. A clump will usually die after flowering. Bamboo serves man in a number of purposes, from food (young sprouts) to building material.

(Left) Alarmed, a spotted deer stag and a fawn gallop for cover.

(Below) The elk-like sambar deer is a highly favored prey for the tiger. Both cat and deer have adopted a similar lifestyle. Living apart, yet together with the opposite sex, they have their peak of activities under cover of darkness and prefer to move in dense jungle.

(Left) In a timeless scene, Sita slips into one of the many carved-out caves that litter the steep slopes of Bandhavgarh fort. According to some Sanskrit inscriptions, it may have sheltered humans since A.D. 300. Temples and statues, overgrown with jungle vegetation, further testify to Bandhavgarh's historic importance as a center of different dynasties. It remained the capital of the ancestors of the present maharaja of Rewa until 1617. Later, the fortress became gradually deserted by man, possibly due to lack of water after continuous years of severe drought. Like several other national parks on the Indian subcontinent, it is probably the protection Bandhavgarh received as a shikar, *or hunting reserve for the royal family and its guests, that saved the forests from the axe. Tribal people, whose culture, tradition, and religion are closely linked with the fort, walk twice a year up the bastion to worship in one of the temples that is still inhabited by a priest.*

(Right) Barka pauses on a forest road for a brief grooming session while patrolling his territory. Walking off moments later at a leisurely pace, he stops to scrape the earth with his hind feet and urinates on the spot. He then sprays his scent against a bush and rubs his neck against a tree trunk. Game trails and nallahs, *or dry river beds, are also extensively used by tigers as a type of network to travel along and establish their territory.*

(Above) The ecological value of endangered wildlife has little meaning for peasants who struggle to make a meager living from the land. This family will spend the night in a watch hut to protect its crops from deer and wild boar. In the day, children move into the cultivated fields to patrol ripening crops.

(Right) Bansore *people, also known as "bamboo weavers," are semi-nomadic tribes that harvest bamboo in the forests, from which they make baskets or other household items. India has a treasure of such tribes whose traditional lifestyles are still deeply rooted in the jungle.*

(Above) A herd of domestic stock is closely followed by cattle egrets. Although not their natural choice, cattle-lifting by tigers can be a serious nuisance. When the number of tigers increases, some dispersing young adults and old or injured tigers find that a cow or a goat grazing along the margins of the forest can be an easy alternative for a meal when natural prey is scarce. Eventually such a tiger could even lose its inborn fear of man and turn into a dreaded man-eater. However, sometimes man himself provokes such incidents by encroaching on a tiger habitat. Intensive grazing damages the land on the periphery of tiger reserves and contributes to soil erosion. When left unattended, domestic cattle and buffalos leave the depleted cultivated fields, tempted to taste the lush vegetation of the protected forests where danger lurks. Cattle may also spread diseases, such as rinderpest, among the wild ungulates.

(Above) The tongues of all cats are covered with strong, sharp papillae, which point backwards—a most effective tool. Fattened up after two days of gorging himself on a wild boar, Nar Bachcha rasps bits of flesh from a bone. After eating, he will lick his coat and bloodstained muzzle and paws with his rough tongue.

(Left) Barka strikes a majestic pose as he straddles a cow he killed in broad daylight. He probably strangled this cow with a throat bite. Unattended, the herd had strayed within the park boundary, and the farmer could not claim any compensation from the government.

(Above) Always on the look-out for an easy meal, Barka suddenly finds the tables turned on him. Returning from a drink in a jungle stream between bouts of feeding, he sees that a jostling mixture of longbilled and whitebacked vultures have crowded in on his kill. Without a second thought, he angrily lashes out at the scavenging group.

(Above) Annoyed by the raucous cries of jungle crows that have gathered near a kill, Balram shakes at a clump of dead bamboo. Early birds, the jungle crows are often the first to detect a carcass, and are thus a reliable source of information for trackers.

(Above) Sita's curled tongue reflects her appetite. With the skill of a surgeon, she has just removed the full stomach from a sambar, before dragging the carcass to thick cover. Later, she will cut through the stomach wall with her carnassial teeth, shake it free, and eat it with relish.

(Left) The tail of a common langur equals its head and body in length. Common langur are wasteful feeders and, especially in the dry season, parties of chital or spotted deer are seen to gather below trees to feed on fruit and leaves that are dropped by the langur. Their close relationship results in an effective warning system against the predators. Langurs have excellent eyesight and profit from their vantage point in the trees. Chital, on the other hand, have well developed senses of hearing and smelling.

(Above) In the midst of summer, a cluster of rocks is the most suitable spot Sita found to hide a sambar hind from scavenging birds and the oppressive heat. The next day, she still lost her quarry to Dao, the pirate.

(Right) Once a large kill is made, like this sambar doe, a tiger will drag the carcass to a secluded, shady spot, preferably close to water. Yet, even then it is not always secure from scavengers and other tigers. Feeding begins at the rump and, using their carnassial teeth for cutting into flesh and skin, tigers gradually work their way to the head. Between feeding bouts, tigers rest near their kill. When they have to leave, they will rake up soil and vegetation to protect their food. Once I saw Sita urinate on a carcass, claiming it for her family, just before leaving to tend her small cubs. As a rule, Sita and her cubs fed in turns on a large kill, possibly to prevent squabbling, or maybe to guard the carcass while the others digested.

(Left) In the midst of summer, Dao lies panting immersed in tall, damp grassland. Even while resting, tigers constantly twist their ears in different directions to pick up the slightest sound. As an alternative to active hunting, a tiger may set up an ambush near a waterhole or close to a game trail, patiently sitting and waiting for a victim who wanders by within striking range.

(Left) In summer, buzzing flies can be pests in wet, damp areas. Perched on a creeper by a river in the forest, an irritated brown fish owl shakes its head violently to get momentary relief from the insects. Its unfeathered legs distinguishes it from the great horned or eagle owl and are well adapted to scoop fish and frogs up from water.

(Above) Tropical, mixed deciduous forest covers much of the upper and southern slopes of the hills in Bandhavgarh. It holds a variety of trees with exotic names like kulu, bahera, amla, haldu, kusum, and pula.

(Left) Balram displays his needle-sharp teeth that will develop into long canines.

(Above) Holding his tail high, Barka sprays as a warning to intruding males. To maintain their exclusive rights, resident tigers have to regularly patrol their territory. An adult male will share his territory with several females and their cubs, who also occupy exclusive areas within that territory. For some time, a resident male may also tolerate transients or young adults who become separated from their mothers. The scent fluid is ejected upwards, hitting the underside of leaves and branches, which keeps it from evaporating too soon.

(Top) Sita has caught such a scent mark. Her tail stiffens with excitement as she indulges in sniffing and licking the marking fluid.

(Below) To examine the message that was left, she hangs her tongue out and wrinkles her nose in a facial expression called "flehmen." The information she receives may give her an idea about the identity or sex of the marker, and whether or not it has recently been sprayed. Chemical signs in the female's marking fluid will advertise when she is in heat.

(Left) Barka suffers a severe cheek wound after a territorial fight. Although he is the apparent victor, the wound may be life-threatening. Though tigers have a well-developed system of communication to avoid such antagonistic confrontations, fatal clashes between tigers of the same sex have been recorded. As a solitary hunter, a tiger cannot afford to be seriously injured. Direct confrontation is usually settled when one animal retreats or shows submission, and such encounters are thought to be very rare.

(Above) The next morning, Barka is still in a daze. His left cheek exposes pink flesh and jaw bones. Clearly unable to keep the gaping wound clean with his long tongue, Forest Department officials decided to tranquilize Barka and stitch it. In his current state, he would not survive long, and the danger of a wounded tiger lingering near human habitation is too high. The festering injury was successfully cleaned and stitched. Luckily, his impressive set of canines was intact, and later Barka fully recovered.

Less than a month after receiving his leg wound, Barka pays Sita a visit, probably attracted to her scentmarks. Initiating the courting ritual, Sita slowly rises and stretches her lean body. Emitting a friendly puffing sound, she circles Barka. They rub heads and shoulders. Though visibly hampered by his limp, Barka nonetheless grabs Sita with a gentle nape bite and straddles her. He maintained his loose grip on her neck fur while they mated briefly. The jungle reverberated when they released each other amid an explosion of snarls.

(Above) Muscular and almost the size of a male, Safeda poses with glossy flanks after cooling off in a muddy pool.

(Above) Deep in the forest, a common kingfisher is on the look-out for little fish in a dancing brooklet.

(Above) A formation of locally migratory cormorants returns from feeding areas to roost for the night on skeleton trees. The trees stand drowned in a water reservoir, built to irrigate farming land adjoining Bandhavgarh.

(Following page) Ever alert to different sounds, Balram detects my presence and sits up from lapping the puddle water, giving me a chance to take this mirror image.